CHOSEN

Understanding Identity and Authority from Ephesians

CINDY W ARORA

ISBN: 978-1-922532-53-4 (Paperback)

 A catalogue record for this book is available from the National Library of Australia

Cover Art: Cindy W Arora
Cover Design: Ocean Reeve Publishing
Design and Typeset: Ocean Reeve Publishing
Printed in Australia by Ocean Reeve Publishing

Published by Cindy W Arora and Ocean Reeve Publishing
www.oceanreevepublishing.com

Foreword

Cindy has done a great job in choosing Ephesians as a guide to helping us all come to a place of intimacy with Jesus. Ephesians' message is to reveal the praise of God's glory in all of us. The word 'glory' in Ephesians refers to the exceeding excellence of God's love for us, as well as His wisdom and power.

If you are looking for greater intimacy with the Lord, this book will lead you to that place. You can go through this book individually or in a group setting.

Your journey to intimacy and healing takes you to testimonies of others who have been healed. It then takes you to a devotional section with a scripture from Ephesians and encouraging words of God's love for you. Then a prayer of thanksgiving to the Lord. The next section leads you to personal reflections of all that you are learning and your healing journal. The last area provides questions for your group to discuss.

When you finish your journey through this book, you will discover your identity as the bride of Christ. You will know Him as your king and your head. You will be positioned as His body and begin to walk into your destiny. No longer an orphan, but a son or daughter loved by your Heavenly Father.

This book will change your life and your relationship with Jesus.

Cal Pierce
International Director
Healing Rooms Ministries

Introduction

Dear reader,

My prayer for you is that you will be drawn into greater intimacy with the Lord, your God. I pray that you are so rooted and grounded in God's love that it becomes *who* you are—your identity.

Each chapter begins with a story of someone's personal experience, perhaps similar to yours. A devotional connects that life experience with the Word of God. I have also included a Personal Reflections and Journaling section to facilitate intimacy with your Beloved. This is your opportunity to experience God through prayer. If you are new to 'listening prayer', I have listed a few tips on the next page—prioritize the Personal Reflection and Journaling section. Savor time in His presence. Rest and reflect. Listen for His voice. Hear His heart for you. Write down anything He reveals to you or anything He says over you. If you need to return to the study questions later because you have spent all your time waiting on God, consider that a great success.

Our identity is in Christ. The Apostle John described himself as 'the disciple whom Jesus loved' (John 13:23). It is not that Jesus loved him more than the other disciples. John felt it was important to declare himself as 'the beloved'. You can make that same declaration: 'I am the beloved!'

Love unlocks the heart and releases peace and freedom. As we continually declare that we are 'the one whom Jesus loves', it becomes the definition of who we are. It becomes our identity. I encourage you to speak the declarations in this book *aloud*, as the Apostle John did. Hearing yourself say these words as a declaration will increase your faith.

In his letter to the Ephesians, the Apostle Paul teaches that believers' identity 'in Christ' impacts every aspect of our lives. Believers all over the world live in a personal, dynamic relationship in unity with the risen Christ! Our identity 'in Him' is crucial for overcoming our former lifestyle, for maintaining Christian unity, for exercising our authority over spiritual darkness, and fulfilling the destiny that God has called us to. Join me as we embrace our identity and authority in Christ from the Book of Ephesians.

To God be the glory!

Cindy

Tips for Listening Prayer

Here are my four tips to enhance your listening prayer. There are also many wonderful books available on contemplative prayer. I highly recommend *Experiencing God Through Prayer* by Jeanne Guyon[1]. Her life story (1648–1717) and writings are inspiring.

1. **Begin with Adoration.** Approach your prayer time with a desire to love God and feel His love for you. He already knows your heart's concerns and the people you love. So, set your list aside and simply tell God how much you love Him and why.

2. **Have a strategy to redirect your mind gently.** Even the most well-trained mind wanders—no need to waste time on negative self-talk. Instead, when you have discovered that your mind is off the topic of the Lord, have a strategy ready. For example, have a psalm open in front of you so that you can read another verse to redirect your mind onto the goodness and glory of the Lord.

3. **Be open to hearing God speak in different ways.** If a Bible story or verse comes to mind, write it down. If a worship song comes to mind, sing it and jot it down. Then ask God why He brought that story or song to mind. Capture thoughts and images that seem to drop out of nowhere. Remember, God gave you an imagination to use for His glory. Note any feelings or emotions, etc. God is wonderfully creative. He speaks in more

1 J Guyon, Experiencing God Through Prayer, Whitaker House, United States of America, 1984

ways than I can list here. Be open to His leading and guiding. If you are unsure, ask Him for confirmation. 'Is that You, God?'

4. **Rest in His presence.** Do not be in a hurry to do the next thing. Relax and simply enjoy His love for you. If we only knew how much God loves us and wants to communicate with us, we would spend all our time waiting on Him.

Contents

Chapter 1: Blessed

Testimony

We were vacationing and on the way to Volcanoes National Park in Hawaii. We had stopped for snacks at a small, local grocery store. As I made my purchase, I noticed a young couple with their baby at the next check stand. The baby looked less than a week old and so cute! The parents were attempting to buy a handful of items with an expired food card. My heart went out to them. I felt the Lord nudging me to purchase their items. But I hesitated, and the opportunity was lost.

Why did I hesitate? Was I anxious to be on my way? Did I feel rushed by the impatient customer behind me? I do not remember. It happened twenty years ago. However, I still remember the missed opportunity to be a blessing to that young family. God has blessed me, and I want to be a blessing.

Another opportunity presented itself this week. I was on the way to pray for a young man with cancer. In the hospital restroom, I came upon a young woman doubled over in pain with tears. Our team ministered God's healing and love to her. As I walked the woman to her car, she shared her struggles to live with her debilitating disease and care for her two preschool children. When we parted, she shed grateful tears and praised God. His hand was clearly on our chance meeting. She could see God's loving care for her and knew He was watching over her. After all, He had sent people to help her and pray for her!

Yes, we also prayed for the young man with cancer. However, I am more convinced than ever that God's opportunities for us to be a blessing happen on the way. So I am more determined than ever to capture those opportunities to be a blessing.

Blessed to be a blessing!

Devotion

'Blessed be the God and Father of our Lord Jesus Christ, who has blessed us with every spiritual blessing in the heavenly places in Christ.'
—Ephesians 1:3

Chapter 1 of Ephesians has become my favorite Scripture passage over the last few years. It lists the spiritual blessings God lavishes on us who are in Christ. I love that word—lavish. It points to the unbelievable richness of the blessings He has gifted us. The richness of those spiritual blessings far outweighs the physical blessings, and they are only found in Jesus Christ.

I love to rehearse the spiritual blessings God has lavished on me. It builds my faith by reminding me who I am in Christ. Those blessings are also my identity. I am chosen by God. I am beloved by God. I am His delightful daughter.

Blessing us was God's purpose and forethought. Before He created the universe, before He ever said, 'Let there be light,' God planned to bless us.

God created man in His own image, and He blessed them (Genesis 1:28). When God wiped the slate clean (with the great flood) and started over with Noah and his family, God blessed them (Genesis 9:1). When God chose Abraham to be the father of the faithful, God blessed him. God also declared that all the Earth's families would be blessed through Abraham (Genesis 12:1–3).

God sought to bless His people again and again. He delivered them from Egypt and led them to His holy mountain, where He made a covenant with them. Moses declared the blessings that would overwhelm Israel if they obeyed God's covenant (Deuteronomy 28:1–14). But they could not. Their sinful nature made it impossible for them to obey.

God knew that. Before the foundation of the world, God knew He would send His Son to free us from the power of sin and death.

How great is the Father's love that He has lavished on us!

Jesus, our Savior from the power of sin, stood on another mountain, declaring a better covenant when he preached on the

Beatitudes (Matthew 5–7). This superior covenant emphasizes an inward transformation of our hearts through grace. No longer is our spiritual blessing dependent on obedience to the law. Praise God!

The Kingdom of God and all its blessings are offered to those who walk with Christ in humility (Matthew 5). God blesses us with the power of His Holy Spirit to do all He asks of us (Acts 1:8). He has also '… blessed us with every spiritual blessing' (Ephesians 1:3). Notice that the verb is past tense. God has already blessed us with everything we need so that we can walk with Him.

God's plans and purposes do not end there. He is working out a grand design in all of human history. God lavished His grace on us so that we could partner with Him in that design. Before we were born, He had a purpose for each of us to fulfil (Jeremiah 29:11). He blessed each of us with a destiny!

Prayer

Father, thank You for Your lavish love. Thank You for every spiritual blessing. Thank You for the privilege of partnering with You to fulfil my destiny. Amen.

Personal Reflections and Journaling

Declaration: God has lavished on me every spiritual blessing. God has given me a destiny.

Make a list of your spiritual blessings in Christ from Ephesians 1.

_____

_____

_____

_____

_____

_____

_____

_____

_____

_____

_____

_____

_____

_____

_____

_____

_____

_____

_____

_____

Declare the previous list *out loud* as your identity in Christ every day for the duration of this study. Record your progress here.

_____

_____

_____

_____

_____

_____

_____

_____

_____

_____

Ask the Father how you can bless others with these spiritual blessings.

_____

_____

_____

_____

_____

_____

_____

_____

Open Your Bible

1. Share a time when you stopped on the way somewhere to be a blessing to someone.

   _____

   _____

   _____

   _____

   _____

   _____

   _____

2. Read Ephesians. Make a list of everything you have 'in Christ' or 'in Him'.

   _____

   _____

   _____

   _____

   _____

   _____

   _____

3.   What is God's purpose in lavishing all these blessings on us?

_____

_____

_____

_____

_____

_____

_____

4.   List those who are the blessed ones in Matthew 5:3–12.

_____

_____

_____

_____

_____

_____

_____

5. Does Jesus' standard in Matthew seem achievable? Why or why not?

_____

_____

_____

_____

_____

_____

_____

6. What insight do the following scriptures explain regarding why God has blessed us? Genesis 12:1–3; 1 Peter 3:8–9

_____

_____

_____

_____

_____

_____

_____

7. Write out the priestly blessing from Numbers 6:22–27.

_____

_____

_____

_____

_____

_____

_____

8. Proclaim (*out loud*) that blessing over your group and family today.

_____

_____

_____

_____

_____

_____

_____

Chapter 2: Chosen

Testimony

Mary was already a grandma with white hair when I met her, and she was one of the most beautiful women in my life. She was a volunteer at the prayer ministry I had just joined. I loved serving on Mary's prayer team because she bubbled over with joy and enthusiasm for the Lord. When she spoke of her Savior, her passion often caught in her throat, and tears welled up in her eyes. At those times, she glowed with the Holy Spirit. Her bright white hair and radiant countenance contributed to her beauty.

One time when I visited her home, Mary showed me pictures of her extended family. I remember thinking how plain and ordinary they looked—even Mary. 'Is that you?' I asked. She laughed. 'Yes, that's before I had white hair.'

It was also a photograph from before Mary met Jesus. The contrast was remarkable. I hardly recognized her. 'You are *more* beautiful with white hair,' I told her. But it was not only the shocking white hair that accounted for her beauty. She also had a joyous glow about her that the younger Mary did not have in the photo.

God chose Mary before the foundation of the world (Ephesians 1:4). He pursued her until she answered His call. She was the first one in her family to commit her life to Jesus. Mary's passion for the Lord kept her praising Him at every opportunity. Slowly, one by one, her whole family came to know the Lord. Mary still praises her Savior to anyone who will stand still for five minutes. That is one of the things that makes her so attractive.

God has chosen each of us to shine forth His glory and His beauty. We are plain and ordinary looking until the 'Light of the World' takes up residence inside us (John 8:12). Then we shine forth His radiance and His beauty. No matter our age, the radiance of God's glory makes us beautiful to behold.

Devotion

'Just as He chose us in Him before the foundation of the world.'
—Ephesians 1:4

You did not choose God. God chose you. Before He spoke the world into existence, God knew He would knit you together in your mother's womb. God is cherishing you in His thoughts every single moment (Psalm 139). God wants to be in a relationship with you. He pursues you like a suitor, speaking kindly and lovingly so that you will turn your face toward Him. There is nothing you can do to earn God's acceptance. He has already chosen you.

This is good news. We live in a world that defines us by our failures and tells us we will never be good enough. Praise God, for we do not have to win His approval or coax Him to love us. He has already chosen us out of His great love toward us. There is nothing we can do to make Him love us more. There is nothing we can do to make Him love us less. Praise God!

Why did God choose us? He chose us so that we would be 'holy and blameless before Him.' Wow! God has lofty plans for us. Before you throw your hands up in despair, be assured that God has given you everything you need to succeed.

Holy means to be 'set apart'. God has set us apart for His purposes. In other words, being 'holy' is a result of God choosing us. We had nothing to do with that. We are simply the recipients of God's love.

On the other hand, being 'blameless' requires something from us. We are required to receive and follow His Spirit. The Holy Spirit makes God's love real to us. The Holy Spirit speaks tender words of affection over us, continually reminding us that we are God's beloved child. The Holy Spirit also teaches us and trains us (John 14:26). As we follow the leading and guidance of the Holy Spirit, God makes us 'blameless.'

God knows we have a sinful nature that fights against our will to follow Him. That is why He has given us His Word and His Spirit. We need to build our faith step by step as we renew our minds to our new identity in Him (Ephesians 4:23).

God also knows we have an enemy who challenges our identity and authority in Christ. The truth of His Word and the power of His Spirit are all we need to prevail against the schemes of the enemy.

Yes, God has given us every spiritual blessing to fulfil His lofty plans for us. Believe what the Bible says about you and your identity in Christ. Never accept failure or defeat as your identity. Renew your mind from the Word. Be attentive to the Holy Spirit. 'For you were once in darkness, but now you are light in the Lord; walk as children of light' (Ephesians 5:8).

Prayer

Thank You, precious heavenly Father, for choosing me just because You love me. Thank You for setting me apart for Your purposes. May I walk as a child of light, radiating Your glory. Amen.

Personal Reflections and Journaling

Declarations: I am chosen by God to be His beloved child. I radiate the light and glory of the Lord.

Meditate on the significance of God choosing you before the foundation of the world. Record your thoughts here.

_____

_____

_____

_____

_____

_____

_____

_____

_____

_____

_____

_____

_____

_____

_____

_____

_____

Ask the Father in what areas you have been allowing the world to define you. Now, write out how God defines you in Christ.

_____

_____

_____

_____

_____

_____

_____

_____

_____

_____

_____

_____

_____

_____

_____

_____

_____

_____

_____

_____

_____

_____

_____

Ask God how can you partner with Him to radiate His glory.

_____

_____

_____

_____

_____

_____

_____

_____

_____

_____

_____

_____

_____

_____

_____

_____

_____

_____

_____

_____

Open Your Bible

1. Name some people in your life who radiate God's light and/ or glory.

_____

_____

_____

_____

_____

_____

_____

2. Why did God choose you (1 Peter 2:4–10)?

_____

_____

_____

_____

_____

_____

_____

3. How might you fulfil that calling?

_____

_____

_____

_____

_____

_____

_____

4. From Isaiah 43:8–13, 20 and 44:1–5, write some declarations to speak over yourself and your family.

_____

_____

_____

_____

_____

_____

_____

5. Read Colossians 3:12–17, listing the virtues with which the chosen are to robe themselves.

_____

_____

_____

_____

_____

_____

_____

6. Which of those virtues do you feel are more difficult than others?

_____

_____

_____

_____

_____

_____

_____

7.   Why did God call you according to 2 Thessalonians 2:13–17?

_____

_____

_____

_____

_____

_____

8.   Where will you shine God's glory this week?

_____

_____

_____

_____

_____

_____

_____

Chapter 3: Holy and Blameless

Testimony

With a heavy heart and glistening eyes, Deborah shared how she had committed adultery and destroyed her marriage thirty years ago. Since then, she had received Christ and succeeded in her second marriage for twenty-five years. Still, her confession produced tears. For years, she struggled to feel forgiven and free. Even today, thirty years later, she occasionally hears accusing voices in her head.

That is so like the enemy of our souls! He ensnares us with temptations and addictions, and then he berates us for falling for them. He constantly makes us feel condemned by reminding us of our mistakes and failings.

However, there is no condemnation for those who are in Christ Jesus (Romans 8:1). Praise Jesus! We do not have to listen to the accuser any longer. Jesus purchased our freedom on the cross. He washed us clean with His blood. We can take off our filthy rags and put on Jesus' robe of righteousness (Isaiah 61:10). We can refuse to entertain the negative messages of the enemy. God has made us holy in Christ, and we are set apart for His purpose. God has given us His Holy Spirit, through whom we can be blameless.

Like my friend, Deborah, perhaps you are still crying over the sins of your past. I encourage you to plug your ears to the lies of the enemy. Receive Jesus' robe of righteousness by putting your faith and trust in Him. Walk in His Spirit so that you will be blameless (Galatians 5:16).

Live in the truth that proclaims, 'I am holy and blameless in Christ!'

Devotion

> *'... that we would be holy and blameless before Him.'*
> —Ephesians 1:4

God declares that we are 'holy and blameless'. That may not be how we feel, but that is who God says we are. Because we are 'hidden in Christ' (Colossians 3:3), when the Father looks at us, He sees His beloved Son.

In the Old Testament, Jacob and Esau's story foreshadowed this blessing of being hidden in Christ. Jacob (the grandson of Abraham) used goat skins to hide his identity (Genesis 27).

Jacob's twin brother, Esau, was born moments before him. That gave Esau all the rights and privileges of the firstborn. When Jacob's father, Isaac, was old and blind, he wanted to bestow upon Esau the blessing of the firstborn. He sent Esau out to hunt and prepare his favorite meal, after which Isaac would pronounce his blessing.

While Esau was out hunting, Jacob and his mother, Rebekah, hatched a plan to deceive Isaac and steal the blessing. Rebekah put Esau's best garments on Jacob so he would smell like Esau. She also put goats' skins on Jacob's hands and neck to disguise him because Esau was a hairy man (and Jacob was smooth-skinned).

Isaac knew his sons' voices, and he suspected the son who brought him the meal was Jacob. Yet, when he smelled the clothing and felt the hairy goatskins, he believed. Isaac pronounced the blessing of the firstborn over Jacob.

As Jacob hid behind the skins of goats, we are hidden in Christ (Colossians 3:3). When Father God looks at us, He sees His beloved Son in whom He is well pleased and pronounces the blessing of the firstborn over us.

However, we are not deceivers like Jacob. Hebrews 10:19 says we can enter the Father's presence with confidence by Jesus Christ's blood. Jesus inaugurated a new and living way for us to come into this holy place through His flesh. Jesus paid a high price so that we might wear His skin with confidence, unlike Jacob, who hid behind goat skins to deceive. Jesus suffered persecution, pain, and death so that we can have access to the Father.

Nor do we have to conspire to steal the Father's blessing like Jacob did. God planned before the foundation of the world to bless us with every spiritual blessing. He has chosen us as His very own, beloved children. God predestined us to adoption, as sons through Christ Jesus, with all the rights and privileges of the firstborn.

God did not spare His own Son but delivered Him up for us all (Romans 8:32). We can remove our past guilt and shame like a discarded garment. We have put on Jesus Christ's robe of righteousness. We are hidden in Him. We are holy and blameless in Him!

Prayer

Thank You, Jesus, for hiding me in Your righteousness. Thank You, Father, for the blessing of the firstborn.

Personal Reflections and Journaling

Declarations: I am holy and blameless. I have the blessing of the firstborn.

Visualize removing your rags of condemnation and putting on Christ's robe of righteousness. Write a prayer of thanksgiving.

_____

_____

_____

_____

_____

_____

_____

_____

_____

_____

_____

_____

_____

_____

_____

_____

Meditate on the blessings of the firstborn. Record your thoughts.

_____

_____

_____

_____

_____

_____

_____

_____

_____

_____

_____

_____

_____

_____

_____

_____

_____

_____

_____

_____

_____

_____

Write a letter to a person in your life who needs to hear this message.

_____

_____

_____

_____

_____

_____

_____

_____

_____

_____

_____

_____

_____

_____

_____

_____

_____

_____

_____

_____

_____

Open Your Bible

1. Are there sins from your past that still make you feel condemned?

_____

_____

_____

_____

_____

_____

_____

2. Read Ephesians 4, listing the old garments to be 'put off' and the new garments to be 'put on'.

_____

_____

_____

_____

_____

_____

_____

3. What is the role of the Holy Spirit in this garment change?

_____

_____

_____

_____

_____

_____

4. Compare Ephesians 4 to the parallel passage in Colossians, Chapter 3. Record your insights on being hidden in Christ.

_____

_____

_____

_____

_____

_____

_____

5. Read Hebrews 10:19–25 in context. How do we live in this 'new and living way?'

_____

_____

_____

_____

_____

_____

_____

6. What are the privileges of being part of 'the church of firstborn' from Hebrews 12:18–29?

_____

_____

_____

_____

_____

_____

_____

7. How can you show gratitude this week for being a part of God's unshakable Kingdom?

_____

_____

_____

_____

_____

_____

_____

Chapter 4: Adopted

Testimony

Before my cousins adopted three-year-old Amaris, she had lived in several different foster homes. Consequently, whenever someone knocked on the door, Amaris assumed she would be thrust into a new living situation. She frantically looked around for something to grab—a toy or a blanket or some article of comfort to cling to. It was heart-wrenching to watch.

For several months after the adoption was final, Amaris still groped for security. Even though she had all the legal rights of adoption, she was not confident in her parents' care. They loved her desperately and did all they could to convince her of their love.

Our heavenly Father loves us desperately too. He does everything He can to convince us of His love. The Father sent His beloved Son to die on the cross so that He could adopt us as His own. I wonder how many of us are still grabbing wildly for security when we have already been adopted. We have all the legal rights and spiritual blessings of adoption, but are we confident of the Father's care? Do we trust that God loves us? Do we trust that He is good?

Amaris slowly grew to trust her new parents. She settled into her place in the family as a beloved and cherished daughter. She has enjoyed her rights and privileges as a daughter for several years. It has been a joy to watch Amaris flourish under the care of loving parents.

How about you? Do you trust God to take care of you? Have you settled into your place as a beloved and cherished child of God? Are you flourishing in His love and blessings?

Devotion

> '*He predestined us to adoption as sons through Jesus Christ to Himself, according to the kind intention of His will.*'
> —Ephesians 1:5

Adoption is a beautiful picture of redemption. God created each of us in our mothers' wombs. In that sense, we are all God's children. However, because of Adam and Eve's sin, we were born into the family of disobedience. God redeemed us from that rebellious family by adoption. Because of Jesus Christ's sacrifice on the cross, God transferred us from the family of sin to the family of His Son (Colossians 1:13). We now live in a blessed Father-child relationship with Father God, thanks to Jesus.

God has enfolded us into His spiritual family. We have all the same rights and privileges as the firstborn Son. We are heirs, not of earthly kings but of God Himself (Romans 8:17). Everything that Christ inherits, we inherit by grace.

Our identity with Father God through Jesus Christ is critically important. Our identity in Christ enables and empowers us to live the victorious Christian life.

Jesus said He could only do what He saw the Father doing (John 5:19). Jesus Christ's authority and power come from His Sonship—His identity with the Father. In turn, our authority and power come from our adoption—our identity with Christ and His Father. Jesus Christ commissioned us to preach the gospel and demonstrate it with signs and wonders (Mark 16:15–20). He delegated His authority and His power to us (Matthew 28:16–20).

Why are we not moving in those signs and wonders? What keeps us from exercising our delegated power and authority? We have an identity crisis. We see ourselves as 'sinners saved by grace'. While that is true, we cannot get stuck wallowing in our sin and brokenness. We need to rise up into our identity and authority in Christ.

The devil challenged Jesus' identity and authority in the wilderness temptations: 'If You are the Son of God ...' (Luke 4:3). In the face of every temptation, Jesus declared the truth of the Word of God. The enemy will also challenge our identity in Christ, hoping to limit our authority in Him. Like Jesus, we need to declare the truth of God's Word in the face of temptation.

We are adopted in Christ as sons and daughters of Almighty God. We walk in Christ's authority. We move in His power. We will do greater things than even Jesus did (John 14:12). This is who we are. This is our identity in Christ!

Prayer

Heavenly Father, thank You for adopting me as Your precious child. Jesus, thank You for trusting me with Your power and Your authority. Holy Spirit, help me to use them wisely for God's glory. Amen.

Personal Reflections and Journaling

Declarations: I am adopted because of God's great love for me. My identity is in Christ Jesus. I am an heir of God in Christ.

Prayerfully consider your answer to the question 'Who are you?'

_____

_____

_____

_____

_____

_____

_____

_____

_____

_____

_____

_____

_____

_____

_____

_____

_____

_____

Reflect on what it looks like to walk in Jesus' power and authority.

_____

_____

_____

_____

_____

_____

_____

_____

_____

_____

_____

_____

_____

_____

_____

_____

_____

_____

_____

_____

_____

_____

How will exercising your power and authority in Christ change your priorities or activities?

_____

_____

_____

_____

_____

_____

_____

_____

_____

_____

_____

_____

_____

_____

_____

_____

_____

_____

_____

_____

_____

_____

_____

_____

Open Your Bible

1. Do you feel you have settled into being a beloved and cherished child of God? Explain your answer.

_____

_____

_____

_____

_____

_____

_____

2. Read about the commissioning of Jesus in Luke 3:21–22. What three things did Jesus need before He entered into ministry?

_____

_____

_____

_____

_____

_____

_____

3. Jesus Christ was tested in the wilderness before He entered into His ministry. How might we be tested?

_____

_____

_____

_____

_____

_____

_____

4. Rewrite the unique aspects from each of our commissioning statements in the four Gospels into one statement: Matthew 28:18–20; Mark 16:15–20; Luke 24:46–49; John 20:21–23.

_____

_____

_____

_____

_____

_____

_____

5. Summarize Paul's arguments in Galatians 4 regarding our adoption as sons.

_____

_____

_____

_____

_____

_____

_____

6. In Galatians 5:1, Paul exhorts us to 'keep standing firm.' How do we do that?

_____

_____

_____

_____

_____

_____

_____

7. How will you proclaim the gospel this week?

_____

_____

_____

_____

_____

_____

_____

Chapter 5: Redeemed

Testimony

Saphir confessed that her addiction had destroyed all her relationships. She lived in her car because she had lost her job and housing. No-one trusted her enough to take her in. In addition to this, Child Protective Services had threatened to take away her four-year-old daughter. As Saphir spilled out her story, she hung her head in shame and hopelessness.

Our prayer team led Saphir to faith in Christ. She was 'born again to a living hope through the resurrection of Jesus Christ from the dead' (1 Peter 1:3). She renounced her association with the addiction and the enemy behind it. We cast that spirit from her, and she was filled with the Holy Spirit. When Saphir lifted her head, we saw relief and hope in her eyes for the first time. We knew complete freedom would take time, but she was no longer alone. Jesus had entered her life, and He would never leave her nor forsake her (Hebrews 13:5).

When we prayed for Saphir, God gave me an image of her as a large block of ice. Inside the block of ice was a small flame, which I equated with the Holy Spirit (Acts 2:3). The small flame was melting her from the inside out.

That is a beautiful picture of how the Holy Spirit transforms each of us from the inside out. God ignites a flame of the Holy Spirit in each of us to draw us into deep intimacy with Himself (Ephesians 3:14–19). The Holy Spirit opens our eyes to the truth (John 16:12–15) and gives us new hopes and desires (Romans 15:13).

Saphir trusted in the truth that Jesus bought her back from the power of sin and death. God ignited a small flame of His Spirit in her heart when she did. She saw a glimmer of hope for the bright future God has for her and for her little girl. There was a glorious celebration in Heaven over Saphir!

Devotion

> *'In Him we have redemption through His blood.'*
> —Ephesians 1:7

God's love for lost people is extravagant. In the parables of Luke 15, we see the extraordinary value God places on every lost soul. The Good Shepherd risked all to search for the one who had strayed. It may have seemed foolhardy for the Shepherd to leave the rest of the flock unattended while He searched for the one. But He did not give up until He finally found the lost sheep. He carried it home, rejoicing. Once home, He invited everyone to come to celebrate the return of the lost lamb.

In the second parable, a woman had ten valuable silver coins. Silver is the symbol of redemption. According to the Old Testament, silver was the price paid for a soul (Leviticus 27:3–6). These particular silver coins in the parable represent ten souls, which are so valuable that Jesus paid for their redemption.

Like the Good Shepherd in the previous parable, the woman celebrated when she found her precious silver coin. She invited all her friends and neighbors to celebrate with her. This is the way God responds every time one precious lost soul repents and turns to Him. He places immeasurable value on every soul. God is ecstatic with joy and calls for a celebration.

You are immeasurably valuable to the Lord. I am immeasurably valuable to Him. He diligently searches for us until we are found.

'The Prodigal Son' is the last of the lost parables. However, this parable is not about a lost sheep who knows nothing about the Father. The 'prodigal' is already a son. He is already in a close, intimate relationship with his father.

Christian, this is you and me! We are already a son or daughter in close, intimate fellowship with the Father. The prodigal son in Christ's parable took his gifts and talents—his inheritance—and insisted on going his own way. He wandered far away from his home and his father. Yikes! Don't you find that disturbing? This could be you. It could be me!

The prodigal son wasted what he had been given on a corrupt lifestyle. He spent everything and ended up with nothing. He became like a branch that cut itself off from the vine (John 15). He had no life source when he turned his back on his father.

A severe famine in that faraway land finally made the prodigal hungry enough to return to his father. Then he was concerned about how his father would receive him. Are you concerned about how the heavenly Father will receive you?

There is no need for concern about how we will be received. Our heavenly Father has ransomed our lives once and for all. We were not ransomed with perishable things like silver and gold. No, God ransomed us with something much more valuable. He purchased our redemption with the precious blood of Jesus, our sacrificial lamb (1Peter 1:18–19).

Our heavenly Father is a loving Father. He longs for us to turn our face to Him so He can be gracious to us. He waits on high to have compassion on us (Isaiah 30:18). Day after day, all day long, He graciously stretches out His hands to us (Romans 10:21). He seeks to redeem *all* who are lost.

Prayer

Thank You, Father, that You place immeasurable value on my soul. Thank You for redeeming me at such a high price. Amen.

Personal Reflections and Journaling

Declarations: I am redeemed! I am celebrated and adored!

Use your imagination to describe the celebration in Heaven when you were redeemed.

_____

_____

_____

_____

_____

_____

_____

_____

_____

_____

_____

_____

_____

_____

_____

_____

_____

_____

Meditate on Matthew 9:13 and record your conversations with the Lord.

Ask the Father where He would have you demonstrate mercy and compassion.

_____

_____

_____

_____

_____

_____

_____

_____

_____

_____

_____

_____

_____

_____

_____

_____

_____

_____

_____

_____

_____

Open Your Bible

1. Have you seen a dramatic 'darkness to light' testimony like Saphir's?

_____

_____

_____

_____

_____

_____

_____

2. Compare and contrast God's provision for 'cleansing' in the Old Covenant and the New Covenant: Numbers 10 versus Hebrews 9:11–28.

_____

_____

_____

_____

_____

_____

_____

3. Express your appreciation for the New Covenant.

_____

_____

_____

_____

_____

_____

_____

4. According to Ephesians 5:22–33 and Romans 12:1–2, how are we transformed into Christ's image?

_____

_____

_____

_____

_____

_____

_____

5. What is the glorious ministry of the Holy Spirit from 2 Corinthians 3:7–18?

_____

_____

_____

_____

_____

_____

_____

6. How do you participate in that glorious ministry of the Holy Spirit?

_____

_____

_____

_____

_____

_____

_____

7.   Where can you participate in this ministry this week?

_____

_____

_____

_____

_____

_____

_____

Chapter 6. Forgiven

Testimony

A speaker at a women's retreat once asked, 'In the light of eternity, does it really matter?' She was attempting to help us let go of offences and move toward forgiveness. I took her advice and forgave the people who had hurt me. By just speaking out, that decision lifted an anvil off my chest. My heart felt so light and free that I took a deep breath—my first breath of 'freedom'.

That breath of freedom gave me a fresh perspective that transformed me from a powerless victim to a victorious overcomer. No longer could the things people do or say control me. I am free to choose my response, and I choose forgiveness!

I choose to forgive because I want to please my God, who commands it (Ephesians 4:32). It is also the best choice for me. It gives no foothold to the enemy in my life, so I can continue to live in freedom. Forgiving keeps me under God's umbrella of protection and blessing. However, it is not always the easiest choice, especially when certain people do not deserve forgiveness. Also, forgiving does not mean forgetting the offence. It simply means that my heart is free of revenge, bitterness, or angst.

When it is difficult to forgive, I have found it helpful to declare my forgiveness aloud. I release the offenders to God's judgment and bless them in Jesus' name. When I forgive this way enough times, my heart eventually follows. This also gives me ammunition when the enemy reminds me of that thing they did or those words they said. I remind the enemy that I have already forgiven them. I am trusting God to defend and protect me.

The women's retreat speaker was right. In the light of eternity, these small offences do not really matter. Seeing through the eyes of eternity has helped me put things into proper perspective. Mountains become molehills in the light of eternity, and puncture wounds become pinpricks.

Looking at life through the eyes of eternity has transformative power!

Devotion

'In Him we have redemption through His blood, the forgiveness of our trespasses, according to the riches of His grace.'
—Ephesians 1:7

Moses pleaded with God in Exodus 33 not to destroy the nation of Israel. The people of Israel had broken their covenant with God. The Israelites had promised to worship and serve only God. They had promised to follow Him and obey Him all the days of their lives. Instead, they created a calf made of gold and offered sacrifices to it (Exodus 32). God was furious! The people's sin was so great that Moses was not sure God would forgive them. So, he offered his own eternal life for their forgiveness (Exodus 32:32).

Who else offered His life for the forgiveness of His people? Christ Jesus. We tend to think that our sins are not as bad as the Israelites' sins in the Old Testament. But Jesus' parable in Matthew 18 clarifies that our 'sin debt' is so enormous that we could not pay it back even if we lived a hundred lifetimes. To be forgiven of our sin debt is our only chance of freedom.

God and Moses continued to discuss how God could be among the nation of Israel again despite their sinfulness. Because of their sin, they would be consumed in the presence of the holy God. This is the problem of sin. It separates us from our holy God.

Like Christ, Moses was acting as the mediator of God's covenant with His people. Moses was saying, 'Look at me and the favor (covenant) that I have with You, not at Your people and their sinful ways (my paraphrase from Exodus 33:13).' Moses was a foreshadowing of Jesus, Who is our Mediator. Jesus Christ is the mediator of a better covenant, which has been enacted on better promises (Hebrews 8). Jesus paid for our rebellion so that we can live in the presence of our holy God. The Father looks at Jesus, His beloved Son, and not at our sin.

Jesus answers the sin problem that God and Moses were discussing. Jesus died on the cross so that there is no question about whether God will forgive us. Forgiveness is already ours.

Our part is to ask for this forgiveness. Accept Jesus as our Mediator. He traded His life for ours. Now, we have access to our holy God. We are free to choose God's blessings. We can settle into being a dearly loved child of God and receive the riches of His grace, which He lavishes on us.

Prayer

Father, thank You for lavishing Your mercy and forgiveness on me. Thank You, Jesus, for being my Mediator. Thank You for my better covenant with You. Amen.

Personal Reflections and Journaling

Declarations: I renew my covenant with the Lord, my God. I am forgiven and free.

Ask the Father if there is anyone you need to forgive. Write it as a declaration.

_____

_____

_____

_____

_____

_____

_____

_____

_____

_____

_____

_____

_____

_____

_____

_____

_____

_____

_____

Pray for an image of the freedom that comes from forgiveness.

_____

_____

_____

_____

_____

_____

_____

_____

_____

_____

_____

_____

_____

_____

_____

_____

_____

_____

_____

_____

_____

_____

_____

Ask the Holy Spirit how you can help others find freedom in forgiveness.

_____

_____

_____

_____

_____

_____

_____

_____

_____

_____

_____

_____

_____

_____

_____

_____

_____

_____

_____

_____

_____

Open Your Bible

1. Who has it been the hardest for you to forgive?

_____

_____

_____

_____

_____

_____

_____

2. Record your insights on forgiveness from Matthew 18:21–35
    and Acts 10:34–48.

_____

_____

_____

_____

_____

_____

_____

3. Where do we need to apply these principles in our world today?

_____

_____

_____

_____

_____

_____

_____

4. List the superior blessings of our new covenant from Hebrews 8:6–13.

_____

_____

_____

_____

_____

_____

_____

5.   How can you show your appreciation for our new covenant?

_____

_____

_____

_____

_____

_____

_____

6.   From 1 John 1, what does your fellowship with God give you?

_____

_____

_____

_____

_____

_____

_____

7. Write a letter of forgiveness. Pray about sending it.

_____

_____

_____

_____

_____

_____

_____

Chapter 7: Enlightened

Testimony

Julia makes stunning jewellery from old silverware. She collects genuine silver flatware from antique stores and flea markets. Some pieces have patterns that she can work into her jewellery designs. But most pieces need to be reshaped into a creative work of art. There is a whole art genre that takes what you and I would call 'junk' and turns it into something beautiful. Julia and other artists salvage broken and discarded items and fashion them into beautiful recreations.

God is the first and ultimate salvage artist. He created the heavens and the earth and everything in them in order to dwell with the people *He created*. But humanity rebelled against God. Now, we and the whole earth groan under the weight of our sin (Romans 8:22). We humans made a mess of things by yielding to the devil the dominion God had given to us. The devil's evil schemes have littered the earth with broken and discarded people. Satan seeks to destroy everything God created.

I have good news! God is going to salvage what looks like junk to us. His original creation was 'good' and 'very good' (Genesis 1:31). God intended, even before the foundation of the world, to redeem His original creation (Ephesians 1:4). Jesus came to recreate what sin had broken. At the end of this age, God is going to recreate the heavens and the earth (Revelation 21:1). He will finally dwell with the redeemed people of His creation, which has been His plan all along. Yes, our God is the ultimate salvage artist!

God is also recreating something beautiful out of you and me. Amen.

Devotion

'In all wisdom and insight He made known to us the mystery of His will, according to His kind intention, which He purposed in Him.'
—Ephesians 1:8–9

God has enlightened us 'in all wisdom and insight'. He has revealed to us who believe in Him the mystery of His will. God delights in baffling the wisdom of the world by saving those who believe in the message of the cross (1 Corinthians 1:21). God's wisdom is to bring us into glory by making us one with Jesus Christ (1 Corinthians 2:7; Ephesians 3:6).

With the death and resurrection of Jesus Christ, the secret (mystery) is out. God intends to redeem and resurrect all people through His only Son, Jesus Christ. *All people* in the vernacular of the Bible is 'Jews and Gentiles'. The whole of the Old Testament hints at this secret. One such hint is found in the resurrection accounts.

The first account in all of Scripture of someone being raised from the dead involves the son of a widowed woman (1 Kings 17). Jobs for women were extremely rare in ancient society, so this son was her only salvation. The prophet, Elijah, prayed, and God resurrected her only son. This shows a picture of God resurrecting His only Son for our salvation. It is also a hint that God intends to save all people, not just the Jews. Why? Because this widow, whose only son was raised from the dead, was a Gentile, not a Jew.

The next instance of resurrection from the dead also includes an only son (2 Kings 4). This time the one being 'saved' is a Jewish woman. God had given her a son as a demonstration of His grace and provision since her husband was old and she had no other children. Alas, the son died, leaving the woman no hope. This time it was the prophet, Elisha, who prayed for the child's resurrection from the dead. This picture is a foreshadowing of Jesus, God's only Son, being raised for our hope and salvation.

These two examples of only sons being raised from the dead are strong hints of the mystery of God. The resurrection of God's only Son is the hope for both Gentiles and Jews. God desires that *all* people come to salvation.

God plans to bring all people and 'all things' together under the headship of Christ Jesus (Ephesians 1:10). However, we currently live in a fallen and fractured world. During Old Testament times, divisions were along religious lines. The Jews were God's chosen people and the keepers of His covenants. All other people were not (Ephesians 2:11–12). Today, the divisions are too numerous to count. People angrily divide over political, racial, and national lines, just to name a few. Unity seems hopeless.

God has revealed to us His plan to recreate humanity into one new man, which is His church (Ephesians 2:15). In His manifold wisdom, God is uniting *all* people—every tongue, every tribe, every nation—into His church. God intends His church to be a beautiful reflection of His colourful creation.

It was Paul's passion to enlighten everyone to God's mystery (Ephesians 3:9). Our confidence in the only Son of God is our hope and our salvation. God's plan for unity is desperately needed in this hour. How can we not share such good news?

Prayer

Thank You, Father, for saving me through Your only Son. Thank You for Your Holy Spirit, Who reveals Your wisdom and insight.

Personal Reflections and Journaling

Declarations: I have all wisdom and insight by God's Spirit.

Ask God to give you a 'before' and 'after' image of His recreation of you.

_____

_____

_____

_____

_____

_____

_____

_____

_____

_____

_____

_____

_____

_____

_____

_____

_____

_____

_____

_____

Meditate on Revelation 5:9–10 in prayer. Record what He shows/
tells you.

_____

_____

_____

_____

_____

_____

_____

_____

_____

_____

_____

_____

_____

_____

_____

_____

_____

_____

_____

_____

How can you partner with God to recreate your family/church/city/ nation?

_____

_____

_____

_____

_____

_____

_____

_____

_____

_____

_____

_____

_____

_____

_____

_____

_____

_____

_____

_____

_____

Open Your Bible

1. Share a time when you recreated a piece of junk into something beautiful.

_____

_____

_____

_____

_____

_____

_____

2. Read Isaiah 11:1–2 in several translations. List the seven attributes of the Holy Spirit.

_____

_____

_____

_____

_____

_____

_____

3. How does knowing these attributes of the Holy Spirit, who lives inside of you, change your life and/or ministry?

_____

_____

_____

_____

_____

_____

_____

4. Read 1 Corinthians 2 in several translations. Explain how every Christian has the mind of Christ.

_____

_____

_____

_____

_____

_____

_____

5. According to Ephesians 4:17–29, what wisdom have we learned from Christ?

_____

_____

_____

_____

_____

_____

_____

6. How might this wisdom be used to recreate our world?

_____

_____

_____

_____

_____

_____

_____

7. How do we live in God's wisdom according to Ephesians 5:15–17?

_____

_____

_____

_____

_____

_____

_____

8. Whom will you enlighten to God's wisdom this week?

_____

_____

_____

_____

_____

_____

_____

Chapter 8: Enriched

Testimony

I had chosen my spot carefully. The sun over my left shoulder flooded the Grand Canyon with light, illuminating the multicolored layers of rock. I settled on a flat rock and withdrew my painting kit from my pack. With water at the ready and a paintbrush in hand, I stared at the Grand Canyon. *Where do I begin? How do I capture the canyon's beauty and grandeur on a tiny piece of watercolor paper?*

I look back now and laugh at myself. I had not taken a single watercolor class at that point. I was so inexperienced that I had taken a child's watercolor set. The set contained only three colors. The paint's quality was so poor that the colors had separated from their binding agent, turning them into a gooey mess. The paintbrush in the set was made from plastic, not even a synthetic sable. What was I thinking? How did I expect to create a masterpiece with such inferior materials?

The Master Artist, who painted the Grand Canyon, is recreating me into His beautiful masterpiece (Ephesians 2:10). He weaves my fiery trials into an intricate tapestry. He rewrites my sufferings into a sonata. He whispers for me to come to join Him in the good works He has prepared for me. God continually takes the gooey mess of my life and creates something beautiful.

You may be wondering how my painting of the Grand Canyon turned out. I did not even bother to finish it. Instead, I headed to the gift shop, where I purchased a colorful photograph of God's beautiful handiwork.

Devotion

'We have obtained an inheritance, having been predestined according to His purpose who works all things after the counsel of His will.'
—Ephesians 1:11

The spiritual blessing of inheritance can be translated in two ways. Both are beautiful. One is that our identity in Christ has enriched us with an inheritance. The other is that God has claimed us as His inheritance.

Yes, God chose us before the foundation of the world to be His recreated people. We are His inheritance. We will be the visible display of His infinite grace and mercy throughout the coming ages. In that sense, we have become God's creative work of art. He is constantly moulding and shaping us through our trials and the good works He has prepared for us. As we fulfil that destiny, we are transformed into His beautiful masterpiece (Ephesians 2:7–10).

God also enriched us with an inheritance. We are co-heirs with Christ (Romans 8:17). All the blessings of the Kingdom of Heaven are available to us in Christ. We have been crowned with a glorious crown—*His* crown (Revelation 3:11).

God clearly states in Isaiah 42:8 that He will not share His glory with another. Why should He? He is Almighty God. He is the One who created the heavens and the earth. He spoke everything into existence by the word of His mouth. He fashioned man from the dust and breathed life into him. Who is like our God? None can compare with Him. He rightly deserves all the glory and all the honor.

Yet, the book of Hebrews states that Jesus brings many sons and daughters to share in His glory (Hebrews 2:10). How can this be? Because in Christ, we are no longer 'another'. We are joined together as 'one' in Christ. We have the great privilege to experience the same unity as God the Father and God the Son, because we are in Christ (John 17:22).

I think we fail to comprehend how impossible and ridiculous this sounds. How can a frail human being, made from the dust of the earth, radiate the blinding glory of Almighty God?

No wonder the religious leaders of Jesus' day were shocked at His blasphemous boastfulness. No wonder unbelievers of today view us Christ-followers incredulously. It is inconceivable! Why would the Creator God choose to dwell inside His created ones?

And yet, here we are. God said, 'I will dwell in them and walk among them' (2 Corinthians 6:16). The spirit that raised Jesus from the dead dwells in us (Romans 8:11). We are crowned with His glory (Hebrews 2:9–10). This is the divine mystery that has now been revealed: Christ in us, the hope of glory (Colossians 1:27).

Beloved, receive your inheritance. Pick up your crown. Put on your new identity in Christ. Reflect God's glory. Radiate His beautiful handiwork in you!

Prayer

Creator God, thank You for enriching me more than I could ever imagine. Thank You that all of Heaven's resources are available to me. Show me how to steward those riches well. Amen.

Personal Reflections and Journaling

Declarations: I am God's beautiful masterpiece. I have an inheritance with the King of kings.

Ask the Father what inheritance (gifts and talents) He has given you.

_____

_____

_____

_____

_____

_____

_____

_____

_____

_____

_____

_____

_____

_____

_____

_____

_____

_____

Ask Him what 'good works' He has planned for you.

_____

_____

_____

_____

_____

_____

_____

_____

_____

_____

_____

_____

_____

_____

_____

_____

_____

_____

_____

_____

What seeds of creativity has God planted in you?

_____

_____

_____

_____

_____

_____

_____

_____

_____

_____

_____

_____

_____

_____

_____

_____

_____

_____

_____

_____

_____

Open Your Bible

1. Did God reveal any latent seeds of creativity in you? Explain.

_____

_____

_____

_____

_____

_____

_____

2. Find the verses from 1 Peter 2:4–10 where God claims you as His own. Write these verses out.

_____

_____

_____

_____

_____

_____

_____

3. Use a concordance or search engine to find other verses where God claims you as His inheritance?

_____

_____

_____

_____

_____

_____

_____

4. From Ephesians 5, how do we inherit the Kingdom of Christ?

_____

_____

_____

_____

_____

_____

_____

5. Make some observations on the Kingdom of Heaven from Matthew 13.

_____

_____

_____

_____

_____

_____

_____

6. Which parable in Matthew 13 is your favorite and why?

_____

_____

_____

_____

_____

_____

_____

7. Pray for God to reveal some creative ways for you to preach the gospel of the Kingdom.

_____

_____

_____

_____

_____

_____

_____

Chapter 9. Sealed

Testimony

Pointing to herself in the photograph, Mara asked, 'Is that me?' Due to her village's remoteness, Mara had never seen her reflection. She recognized other family members in the photograph then realized that the face she had never seen before must be her own.

What would it be like to never have seen your reflection in a mirror?

I imagine it would be freeing. Most of us do not like what we see in the mirror because we measure ourselves by the world's standard of beauty. If that is the case, we are looking into the wrong mirror.

James, Chapter 3, says that the word of God is our mirror. From the mirror of the word, we can discover how God sees us—our identity in Christ. Unfortunately, we go out into the world and forget our divine origin.

God has recreated us through Jesus Christ's death and resurrection. God has sealed us with His Holy Spirit of promise (Ephesians 1:13). How radiant and glorious is this new ministry of the Holy Spirit within us! As we draw close to the Holy Spirit, *we* become the mirrors. We reflect the glory of the Lord Jesus (2 Corinthians 3:7–18). As we live out our identity in Him, we ourselves are being transformed into His beautiful image. We are growing from glory to glory.

Gaze into the mirror of God. Behold the Beautiful One. Then you will reflect His glory—His beauty.

Devotion

'In Him, you also, after listening to the message of truth, the gospel of your salvation—having also believed, you were sealed in Him with the Holy Spirit of promise.'

—Ephesians 1:13

In Exodus 28, God specifically details the Old Testament priests' garments. He told Moses to '… make a plate of pure gold and engrave on it, like the engraving of a seal, "Holy to the Lord"' (Exodus 28:36). Aaron, the high priest, wore this 'seal' in the form of a gold plate on his turban, across his forehead. Aaron wore the seal that said he was 'Holy to the Lord'.

This caught my attention because we, like Aaron, are priests for God (1 Peter 2:9). We have been sealed with the Holy Spirit for the day of redemption (Ephesians 4:30). The Holy Spirit makes us 'holy to the Lord.'

A seal is used for different purposes. The seal on a letter or document indicates authenticity and ownership. The seal of the Holy Spirit on us indicates ownership too. We belong to God. That is what the word *holy* means, 'to be set apart.' Our seal declares to the spirit realm that we are holy—set apart—to the Lord.

A seal also provides legitimacy and authority. An ambassador was a recognized authority when he carried the king's seal. You and I carry the seal of the King of kings. We are Christ's ambassadors. We carry His delegated authority. We are set apart for His service.

Finally, a seal provides security and preservation. Twice in Scripture, God sent an angel to place a seal on the foreheads of His faithful servants (Ezekiel 9; Revelation 7). That seal protected them in the coming judgment. Our seal also protects us from the coming judgment.

God had security and preservation in mind in Exodus 28. In connection with the seal, God said Aaron shall 'take away the iniquity' so that 'they may be accepted before the Lord' (Exodus 28:38). Here, Aaron, as high priest, was a foreshadowing of Jesus Christ, our Great High Priest (Hebrews 5). Jesus Christ takes away our iniquity so that we may be accepted before the Lord. He also seals us with the Holy Spirit. Across our foreheads an unseen seal blazes—'Holy to the Lord.'

Security and preservation were also what Paul was implying in Ephesians 4:30. The Holy Spirit is keeping us for the day of redemption. The image of God sealing us with His Holy Spirit incorporates all these meanings—authenticity, authority, and security. Until that day of redemption, we continually grow from glory to glory in Jesus Christ.

Prayer

Father, thank You for Jesus, who makes me acceptable in Your sight. Thank You for sealing me with Your Holy Spirit. Amen.

Personal Reflections and Journaling

Declarations: In Christ, I am acceptable to the Lord. I am sealed with the Holy Spirit. I am growing from glory to glory.

Spend some time gazing into the mirror of God's Word (Ephesians 1–3). Write your reflections here.

_____

_____

_____

_____

_____

_____

_____

_____

_____

_____

_____

_____

_____

_____

_____

_____

_____

_____

Visualize yourself with 'Holy to the Lord' sealed on your forehead. How might that change your life and ministry?

_____

_____

_____

_____

_____

_____

_____

_____

_____

_____

_____

_____

_____

_____

_____

_____

_____

_____

_____

_____

_____

Where can you help others choose God's mirror?

_____

_____

_____

_____

_____

_____

_____

_____

_____

_____

_____

_____

_____

_____

_____

_____

_____

_____

_____

_____

_____

_____

_____

Open Your Bible

1. How does your idea of a priest differ from God's?

_____

_____

_____

_____

_____

_____

_____

2. Read Exodus 28. What is God's stated purpose for the priest's garments (hint: verse 2 and 40)?

_____

_____

_____

_____

_____

_____

_____

3. What other garments from Exodus 28 might we want to 'put on' as New Testament priests?

_____

_____

_____

_____

_____

_____

_____

4. At what point does the seal of the Holy Spirit take place? John 7:37–39; Acts 2:38–39.

_____

_____

_____

_____

_____

_____

_____

5. Read Matthew 3:7–12 and Acts 2:1–4. What are the similarities and differences between being baptized with the Holy Spirit and being baptized with fire?

_____

_____

_____

_____

_____

_____

_____

6. How might these differences impact your life?

_____

_____

_____

_____

_____

_____

_____

7. From Ephesians 4:31, list the things that grieve the Holy Spirit and their opposite.

_____

_____

_____

_____

_____

_____

_____

8. Pray through the list above; confess and repent of anything the Holy Spirit highlights.

_____

_____

_____

_____

_____

_____

_____

Chapter 10: Promised

Testimony

I held the phone to my ear and wondered how to respond to Sheva's complaints about our church's leadership. Nothing I said would convince her to stay in our congregation. She and her family had attended—and rejected—every major church in our area.

Many other families, ones who had attended our church for years, were leaving too. These were sisters and brothers with whom I had a shared life. We had sought the Lord together in Bible studies and through prayer. We had parented our kids together. We had laughed and fellowshipped together. I was grieved to see them go.

A change in the church's leadership had caused this ripple. The new direction and emphasis rankled many long-time members. I was careful not to gossip or complain. I knew what the Word says about that! Yikes! Still, I wondered if I should leave too.

I prayed anxiously for weeks. I asked God what He thought of the new emphasis of our church. Were we headed in a dangerously compromising direction? Should I find a new church home? If so, which one?

God's answer made me laugh. 'Row or get out of the boat.'

My job was to row in unison with the other oarsmen or get out of the boat. God seemed to be saying that in this instance: unity was more important than direction. It did not matter if I agreed with the person whose hand was on the rudder. My job was to build unity.

God promises a blessing on brothers and sisters who live together in unity (Psalm 133). I want to live in the promises of God. I want to live in the blessing and favor of God. I chose to row.

Devotion

'You were sealed in Him with the Holy Spirit of promise, who is given as a pledge of our inheritance, with a view to the redemption of God's own possession, to the praise of His glory.'
—Ephesians 1:13–14

God gave us His Holy Spirit as a pledge, a betrothal gift, of our future inheritance. All the spiritual blessings we have been given are just a small fraction of our true inheritance. God has promised us the redemption of our bodies (Romans 8:23), an opportunity to reign with Christ (2 Timothy 2:12), a marriage supper (Revelation 19), a new heaven, a new earth (2 Peter 3:13), and so much more!

Christ Jesus ascended into Heaven to begin the restoration of all things (Ephesians 4:10). Soon, Jesus will appear again to fulfil His every promise (Hebrews 9:28).

In the meantime, God has called us into unity—unity in Christ and unity with each other. Jesus Christ gave us His glory so that we may be in perfect unity, just like God the Father and God the Son. Our unity should demonstrate to the world that out of His love, God sent Jesus for them (John 17:23).

Unity is the chief aim of equipping the saints for the ministry (Ephesians 4:13). God established unity and peace by recreating 'one new man' (the church) in Christ Jesus. We are called to diligently preserve that unity (Ephesians 4:3). Everything we do, every word we say, every attitude of our hearts must diligently guard the unity God has established. Love is the mantle that we wear that brings about unity (Colossians 3:14).

Our lofty position in Christ and our promise of future inheritance compels us to walk in a manner worthy of His call upon our lives (Ephesians 4:1). We need to lay aside our old identity and its misdeeds. We need to embrace the glorious Christ within—our new identity in Christ. God has already recreated us in His likeness. We walk out that new identity by yielding to our new life in Christ, by adorning ourselves with garments of glory and beauty, and by living in God's love (Ephesians 4:24).

Love is how the world will know we belong to Him (John 13:35). That is why unity is so key in the body of Christ. We want the watching world to see a unity and love that is attractive.

Jesus is returning soon. He is coming to collect His beautiful bride (the church), one that lives in unity and love. Are we ready?

Prayer

Thank You, Father, for Your promise of a future inheritance. I look forward to an eternity with You. In the meantime, may I show forth Your love and unity. Come, Lord Jesus, come!

Personal Reflections and Journaling

Declarations: I am a child of promise. I have a new identity. I live in the favor and blessing of God.

Spend some time repenting of times when you undermined unity in your family, church, etc.

_____

_____

_____

_____

_____

_____

_____

_____

_____

_____

_____

_____

_____

_____

_____

_____

_____

Meditate on your promise of your future inheritance. Express thanks to Him.

_____

_____

_____

_____

_____

_____

_____

_____

_____

_____

_____

_____

_____

_____

_____

_____

_____

_____

_____

_____

_____

Ask the Lord for some creative ways to encourage others toward love and unity.

_____

_____

_____

_____

_____

_____

_____

_____

_____

_____

_____

_____

_____

_____

_____

_____

_____

_____

_____

_____

_____

Open Your Bible

1. Has God ever spoken a clear word to you regarding your
    church?

    _____

    _____

    _____

    _____

    _____

    _____

    _____

2. Read 2 Peter and restate, in your own words, his assertions
    about the promises of God.

    _____

    _____

    _____

    _____

    _____

    _____

    _____

3. How shall we live in the light of those promises?

_____

_____

_____

_____

_____

_____

_____

4. Paul uses several metaphors for unity in Ephesians 4 & 5. The family is one. What are some others?

_____

_____

_____

_____

_____

_____

_____

5. Which metaphor is your favorite and why?

_____

_____

_____

_____

_____

_____

6. Summarize how one can walk in unity from the following scriptures: Romans 5; Galatians 5; Ephesians 4; Hebrews 6:9–20.

_____

_____

_____

_____

_____

_____

_____

7.   What will you do this week to answer the call to unity?

_____

_____

_____

_____

_____

_____

_____

Chapter 11: Seated

Testimony

David came to our healing rooms in so much pain that he wore a compression belt on his back. No injury had precipitated the pain, but he had struggled with it for weeks. With a toddler and a baby, David needed a strong back to care for his children.

Our prayer team commanded the pain to leave and blessed David with God's promises and destiny. Immediately, the pain left him. David walked out of the room with his compression belt in his hand and a smile on his face.

On the drive home, David's back pain returned. He commanded the pain to go away, and it did. However, the pain returned. Again, he commanded it to leave, and the pain receded. Then the pain returned yet again. Ten times David had to command the pain to go away before it left and never returned.

Healing is part of the price Jesus paid for us on the cross (Isaiah 53:4–5). Physical healing is a confirmation of God's covenant with us (Hebrews 2:3–4). The enemy wants to steal, kill, and destroy all that God has given us. Sometimes, healing is about taking authority over the enemy (Matthew 8:5–13). We must take our sword, which is the Word of God, and stand our ground (Ephesians 6:10–17).

Devotion

'But God, being rich in mercy, because of His great love with which He loved us, even when we were dead in our transgressions, made us alive together with Christ (by grace you have been saved), and raised us up with Him, and seated us with Him in the heavenly places in Christ Jesus.'
—Ephesians 2:4–6

Ephesians, Chapter 2, takes us from death to life. We were spiritually dead in our trespasses and sins, but God made us alive together with Christ. God also raised us up with Christ at His ascension and seated us with Christ in the heavenly places.

From this lofty position, we live in two realms, simultaneously. We are fleshly beings living on the earth in a mortal body. We are also spiritual beings seated with Christ at the Father's right hand. Because we are seated with Christ, we live in His power and His authority. We are in the unique position to bring God's Kingdom here on the earth.

God created us to rule and reign on the earth. God gave Adam and Eve dominion over the earth and everything in it (Genesis 1:28). Unfortunately, Adam yielded to the enemy and gave his authority over to Satan. No-one reigns over the one to whom they yield. This is the reason God tells us to resist the devil, and he will flee from us (James 4:7). In other words, exercise your authority over him, and he must flee.

It is still God's plan for the people of His creation to rule and reign (Romans 5:17). Jesus came to the earth to purchase back that authority for us. He did not come to get authority back for Himself. He was already ruling and reigning in Heaven. In fact, He emptied Himself that we might be filled with His fullness (Philippians 2:7). He came so that you and I could have authority over all the works of the devil (Luke 10:19). Jesus Christ's death on the cross disarmed and triumphed over the rulers of darkness (Colossians 2:15).

Yet, Satan acts like he continues to reign. He kills people with disease and accidents. He steals people's children and resources.

He destroys people's homes and relationships. However, Satan has no real authority here. He rules through fear and intimidation.

You and I were created to have dominion. Jesus paid a high price to purchase this authority for us. Every believer has authority in Jesus' name. His precious name carries full authority, and we have His delegated authority. Therefore, we can pray for the sick and see them healed. We can cast out demons, and they must go. Jesus' authority! Jesus' power! We are co-laboring with Him.

God is raising an army of believers who will take Him at His word and use His authority to bring His Kingdom here on the earth. Because we are seated with Christ in the heavenly realm, we have the right—the authority—to speak declarations and decrees from His word.

Truth, righteousness, peace, faith, salvation, and the Word of God, are spiritual blessings that God has already given us (Ephesians 6:14). We are prepared for whatever spiritual battles lay ahead. We are told to 'stand firm' (Ephesians 6:11) and pray. There is no need to fight in the natural world. Prayer is the battlefield, and God's Word is our weapon!

Rise up in the supernatural strength of Jesus Christ. Stand victoriously with His weapon of truth. Allow His power to flow in you and through you. This is how we move mountains. This is how we heal the sick. This is how we raise the dead. This is how we cast out demons.

This is our identity in Christ!

Prayer

Father, thank You for giving me all things in Christ. Grow me up into my identity and authority in Christ. Use me for Your glory. Amen.

Personal Reflections and Journaling

Declarations: I am seated with Christ in the heavenly realm. God has given me dominion over the earth and everything in it. I will reign in life through Jesus Christ.

Ask the Father for some declarations to speak over yourself.

_____

_____

_____

_____

_____

_____

_____

_____

_____

_____

_____

_____

_____

_____

_____

_____

_____

_____

How would He have you exercise your authority in Christ?

_____

_____

_____

_____

_____

_____

_____

_____

_____

_____

_____

_____

_____

_____

_____

_____

_____

_____

_____

_____

_____

_____

Ask for some declarations to speak over your family/church/city/ nation.

_____

_____

_____

_____

_____

_____

_____

_____

_____

_____

_____

_____

_____

_____

_____

_____

_____

_____

_____

_____

Open Your Bible

1. Have you ever encountered a healing that was more spiritual than physical? Explain your experience.

_____

_____

_____

_____

_____

_____

_____

2. List the qualities of those whose prayers are answered: Matthew 21:18–22; Mark 11:22–24; Romans 4:6–25; Hebrews 11:3–7.

_____

_____

_____

_____

_____

_____

_____

3. Describe a situation in your life that was resolved only through prayer.

_____

_____

_____

_____

_____

_____

_____

4. What practical evidence of being seated with Christ do you find from Ephesians 4?

_____

_____

_____

_____

_____

_____

_____

5. List the Messiah's garments from Isaiah 11:1–5.

_____

_____

_____

_____

_____

_____

_____

6. Compare the Messiah's garments in Isaiah 11 to the garments of Ephesians 6.

_____

_____

_____

_____

_____

_____

_____

7. Where will you use your spiritual weapons this week?

_____

_____

_____

_____

_____

_____

_____

Chapter 12: Loved

Testimony

My precious Lord used a treasured memory to give me a glimpse of His unfathomable love for me. He brought to my remembrance the following scene.

One day, when my seven-year-old daughter was playing contentedly, I announced that I had to go somewhere. I gave her the option of staying at home with her father or going with me. She whirled her anxious face to me and blurted, 'Mommy, I want to be *with* you, and I want to be *like* you!'

Tears spring to my eyes even now, as they did then, at her innocent, pleading devotion. It is a treasured memory that touches the tenderest place in my heart. A smile always lingers on my lips even as the memory fades.

God brought that memory to mind for a purpose. I prayed the same innocent, pleading devotion. 'Lord, I want to be *with* you. And I want to be *like* you.' God delights in simple, innocent, child-like faith.

There is more. God's still, small voice inside of me said, 'Yes, my daughter, just as you treasure your daughter's devotion, so I treasure yours. It touches the tenderest place in My heart. It brings tears to My eyes and a smile to My lips to hear you express your love to Me.'

Wow! God delights in my devotion. He looks upon me with the tenderness of a Father toward His beloved daughter. Knowing that my devotion pleases the Father's heart fills my heart with even greater devotion and love. Just knowing that I love Him blesses Him. What a beautiful glimpse of my Father's heart!

Devotion

'So that Christ may dwell in your hearts through faith; and that you, being rooted and grounded in love, may be able to comprehend with all the saints what is the breadth and length and height and depth, and to know the love of Christ which surpasses knowledge, that you may be filled up to all the fullness of God.'

—Ephesians 3:17–19

Because of Jesus Christ's death on the cross, we have the great privilege and delight to have a personal and intimate relationship with the God of the universe.

Christ's love for us is deeply intimate. His love for us soars higher than the highest heights. His love for us extends beyond our reach. In us and for us, his abiding love is vast—without measure. God's love truly is endless. He wants us so rooted and grounded in His infinite love that it becomes our identity. I am loved!

When my God endlessly loves me, then I am not chasing after fickle and fading human love. When I am endlessly loved, it is easy to forgive offences. My God has been gracious to me; I can afford to be gracious to others. When I am endlessly loved, I radiate a deep and abiding joy, even in difficult circumstances. When I am endlessly loved, the glory and beauty of the Lord exude from me.

My identity is 'I am loved'. My identity is also 'I reflect love'. This is a bold statement. Christ dwells in my heart and fills me to the fullest with God's endless love. His supernatural love fills me and overflows, splashing out onto those around me. I am a fountain of His endless love. I reflect love.

God is looking for those who will pursue a greater revelation of His love and find their identity there. God is calling us into our identity. 'I am loved!' God is calling us into our destiny. 'I reflect love!'

We were created to live with God's endless love radiating from us so that the world will see who He is. God is love. We are the gates that release love, forgiveness, joy, beauty, and all the other blessings of the Kingdom of God. This is who we are. This is our identity in Christ.

Prayer

Precious Father, thank You for calling me deeper into Your endless love. Grow me into my destiny. Release Your beautiful Kingdom through me. Amen.

Personal Reflections and Journaling

Declaration: I am loved. I reflect love.

Declare your love and devotion to God. Wait for His response.

_____

_____

_____

_____

_____

_____

_____

_____

_____

_____

_____

_____

_____

_____

_____

_____

_____

_____

Meditate on Ephesians 3:20 and imagine wild dreams with God.

_____

_____

_____

_____

_____

_____

_____

_____

_____

_____

_____

_____

_____

_____

_____

_____

_____

_____

_____

_____

_____

_____

_____

Ask God where He would have you reflect His love.

_____

_____

_____

_____

_____

_____

_____

_____

_____

_____

_____

_____

_____

_____

_____

_____

_____

_____

_____

_____

_____

_____

_____

Open Your Bible

1. Share a time when you felt endlessly loved by God.

_____

_____

_____

_____

_____

_____

_____

2. Compare the superlative language in these passages and record your insights: John 15:1–17; Romans 8:31–39; Ephesians 3.

_____

_____

_____

_____

_____

_____

_____

3. When have you felt like more than a conqueror through Christ?

_____

_____

_____

_____

_____

_____

_____

4. How is God's love perfecting us (1 John 4 and 5)?

_____

_____

_____

_____

_____

_____

_____

5. Rewrite 1 Corinthians 13:4–7 with your name in place of the word 'love.' Speak it out loud.

_____

_____

_____

_____

_____

_____

_____

6. List some practical ways to show love from Ephesians 4 and 5.

_____

_____

_____

_____

_____

_____

_____

7. Think of someone who needs the message of this book. Gift them a copy today.

_____

_____

_____

_____

_____

_____

_____

Your Testimony

We would love to hear what God is doing in and through your life during this study.

Did you hear God in a new way? Please share it with us!

Do you move in more power and authority? We would love to rejoice with you!

Have your declarations transformed your life and/or family? Let us celebrate with you!

Contact us:
Email – Cindy.Reflectionsonbeauty@gmail.com
Instagram – cindy.reflectionsonbeauty
Facebook – Cindy Arora
USPS – PO Box 3394, Redmond, WA 98073, USA
Website – www.reflectionsonbeauty.com